I0996079

Also available
by Laurence and Catherine Anholt

Sun Snow Stars Sky
All About You
One, Two, Three, Count With Me
Look What I Can Do

by Catherine Anholt
When I Was a Baby
Tom's Rainbow Walk

For all the children at Uplyme Village School

ANIMALS ANIMALS

All Around

ANIMALS ANIMALS
All Around

Catherine and Laurence Anholt

Animals, animals all around,
high in the sky
and low on the ground.
In the tops of trees,
in rivers and seas,
even deep down underground.

Which animals can YOU see?

Look! Animals have all kinds
of marks.

Some are spotty, like leopards,
giraffes, dalmatians and deer.

Some have stripes, like zebras,
tigers, racoons and bees.

Others have all kinds of colours,

like parrots, peacocks,
butterflies and chameleons.

Animals feel different when you touch them.

Rabbits, kittens, puppies, chicks
and baby bears feel soft.

Fish, crocodiles, lizards
and snakes feel scaly.

Hedgehogs and porcupines feel prickly.

Slugs and snails are slimy.

Rhinos, elephants and hippos feel rough.
Which animal would YOU like to stroke?

Listen! Animals make all kinds of noises.

Lions roar,

dogs bark,

birds sing,

snakes hiss,

horses neigh

and frogs croak.

Sheep baa,

pigs grunt,

elephants trumpet,

cows moo,

ducks quack

and owls hoot.

Which sounds can YOU make?

These animals are still babies.

piglets

foals

kids

puppies

cygnets

ducklings

kittens

chicks

calves

lambs

cubs

tadpoles

What will they be called when they grow up?

Each animal has its own way of moving.

Kangaroos and rabbits jump.

Worms and caterpillars crawl.

Whales and dolphins swim.

Koalas and monkeys climb.

Birds and bats fly.

What can YOU do?

Some animals are fast.
Cheetahs chase,

deer dash,

scorpions scuttle,

hares hurry

and zebras zoom.

Others animals are very slow.

Penguins plod,

warthogs waddle,

donkeys dawdle,

tortoises trudge

and sloths just sleep.

Do you know what animals eat?

Lions and tigers munch meat.

Donkeys and goats graze on grass.

Spiders and toads feed on flies.

Rabbits and caterpillars love leaves.

Birds and squirrels nibble nuts.

What would you choose for YOUR dinner?

Some animals make good pets.
Others are far too scary.

crabs

crocodiles

cats

rhinos

rabbits

rats

deer

doves

dogs

horses

hamsters

hogs

wolves

wallabies

whales

sea lions

snakes

snails

ferrets

foxes

fleas

bears

buffalo

bees

Which animal would YOU like to take home?

Where do animals sleep?

Badgers snooze in sets,

moles hide in holes,

snails slumber in their shells,

birds nap in nests,

squirrels doze in dreys,

bears creep into caves,

toads snore under stones,

alligators rest in rivers,

lions dream in dens

and children bounce into bed –
with their favourite animals!

First published in Great Britain 1998
by Mammoth
an imprint of Reed International Books Ltd
Michelin House, 81 Fulham Road, London SW3 6RB
10 9 8 7 6 5 4 3 2
Copyright © Catherine and Laurence Anholt 1998
Catherine and Laurence Anholt have asserted their moral rights
ISBN 0 7497 3024 2

A CIP catalogue record for this title is available from the British Library

Produced by Oriental Press Ltd
Printed and bound in the U.A.E

This paperback is sold subject to the condition
that it shall not by way of trade or otherwise,
be lent, resold, hired out, or otherwise circulated
without the publisher's prior consent in any form
of binding or cover other than that in which
it is published and without a similar condition
including this condition being imposed
on the subsequent purchaser.